INTRODUCTION

infinite romance

Feisty, independent tomboy Kristen Stewart has been
a professional actress since she was just nine years
old. Although she made her big break playing Jodie
Foster's daughter in *Panic Room*, she starred in a
number of low key indie flicks before getting the role
that would catapult her to superstardom: winning our
hearts as the modest teenage heroine Isabella 'Bella'
Swan in the *Twilight* saga.

That's not all we've got to thank Kristen for. After being cast as Bella, the young actress was responsible for Robert Pattinson's inclusion in the film, refusing to play the part unless he was cast opposite her. And for that, legions of screaming girls across the world thanked her!

As well as fighting off the rumours about her and her vampire lover, Kristen has managed to fit in shooting a number of other films, touring the world promoting the Twilight series, making her way to the front covers of countless magazines, and taking on the role of fashion icon for a whole generation – not only in her own classic way on the red carpet, but also with the prep-indie tomboy chic of Bella.

This is one busy young lady! But who is the real Kristen Stewart? Follow us as we delve into her past, explore her fashion and style sense, and uncover all the Twilight secrets!

KRISTEN ON HER AMBITIONS:

"Usually when people ask me what kind of movies I want to make, I'm like, 'I don't know, good ones.'"

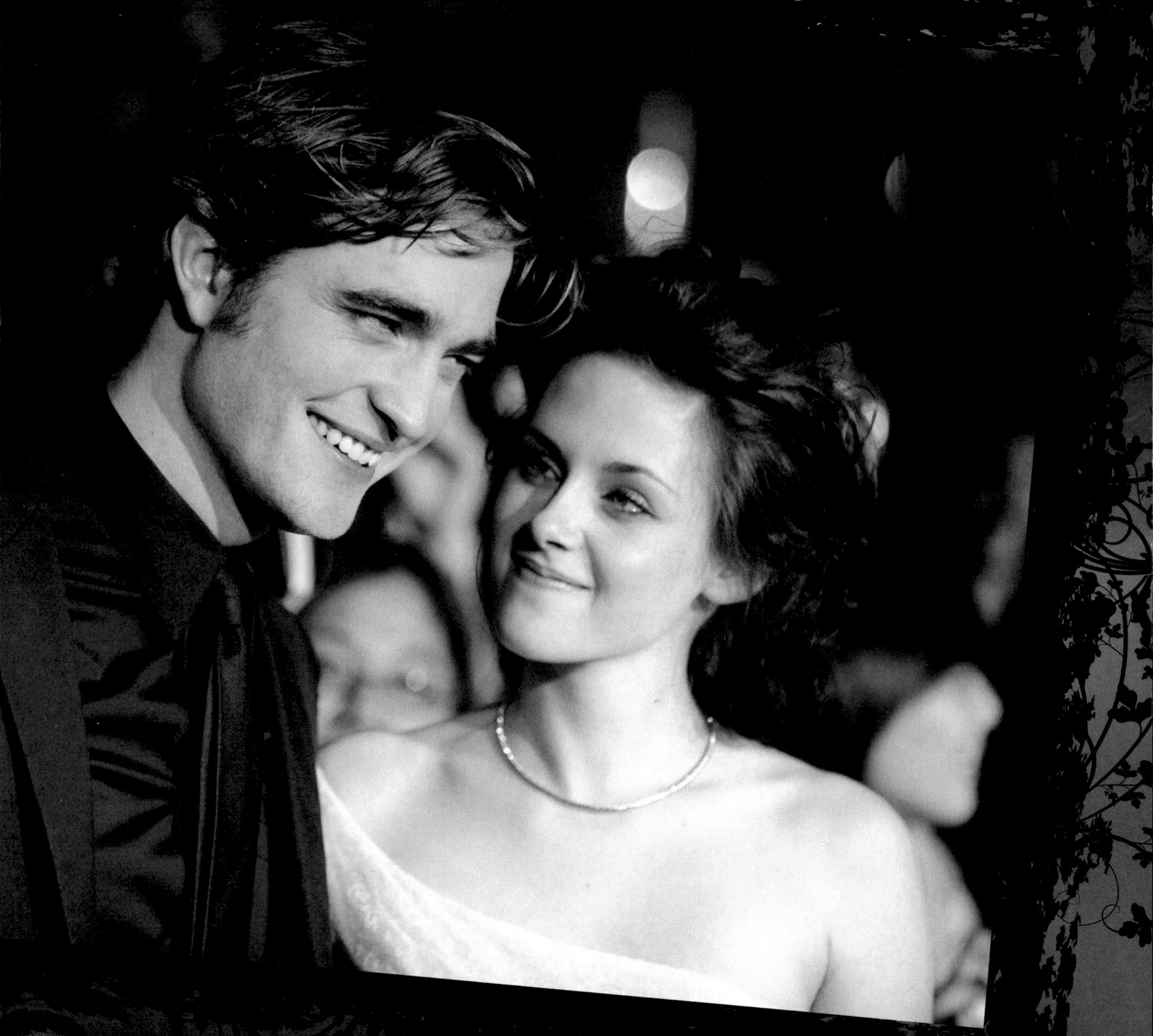

CHAPTER 1
meet kristen

BIRTHDAY: 9 April 1990

BIRTHPLACE: Los Angeles, California, USA

FULL NAME: Kristen Jaymes Stewart

NICKNAMES: Kris, KStew

HEIGHT: 5 feet 6 inches (1.68 m)

ZODIAC SIGN: Aries

EYE COLOUR: Green

HAIR COLOUR: Brown

RELATIONSHIP STATUS: Has been with boyfriend Michael Angarano for two years

PETS: Three dogs – Oz, a border collie mix, and Jack and Lily who are mutts – as well as a cat named Jella

FAVOURITE FILMS: *American Beauty, The Shining, ET, Spaceballs*

FAVOURITE ACTRESSES: Jodie Foster, Evan Rachel Wood, Natalie Portman

FAVOURITE ACTORS: Emile Hirsch, Robert De Niro

FAVOURITE DIRECTORS: Martin Scorsese, Michael Gondry

FAVOURITE AUTHORS: Charles Bukowski, Kurt Vonnegut Jr

FAVOURITE BOOK: *East of Eden* by John Steinbeck and *The Stranger* by Albert Camus

AWARDS: Has been nominated for a Young Artist Award five times, and in 2008 was ranked #17 on Entertainment Weekly's '30 Under 30' hot list

ROLE MODEL: Her grandma, "for her strength and resilience"

HOBBIES AND INTERESTS: Travelling, surfing, writing (went through a poetry phase, and at one point wanted to write a novel or screenplay)

all about kristen

It's as if Kristen Stewart was destined to be famous. She comes from a totally showbiz family – her grandfather was Cecil B. DeMille's assistant director, her father John is a producer, her mum Jules is a screenwriter and brother Cameron has worked as a grip. Must be something in the Stewart blood!

Born on 9 April 1990 in Los Angeles, Kristen's family moved briefly to Colorado before returning to LA, where her dad, John, worked as a stage manager, producer and director on some television shows. When Kristen was performing in a junior school Christmas play, she caught the eye of an agent in the audience, who contacted Kristen's parents to see if she was interested in becoming an actress. Both her mum and dad were opposed to the idea, but Kristen won them over and at just eight-years-old she began auditioning for film and television roles.

Kristen loves scary films. She says, *"I love horror movies that make you think instead of using loud noises to scare you."*

Her first screen appearance was a small part in the Disney Channel production, *The Thirteenth Year*. But rather than going down the Disney route she wanted more serious roles, and got her big break playing Jodie Foster's daughter in 2002's *Panic Room*, a role that was originally supposed to be played by Hayden Panettiere.

She starred in several more films, including *Speak, Fierce People, The Messengers, Into the Wild, The Cake Eaters* and *What Just Happened*, before landing the role that was to change her life – Isabella 'Bella' Swan in the film adaptation of Stephenie Meyer's novel, *Twilight*.

At the time, Kristen was shooting another movie, *Adventureland*, when *Twilight* director Catherine Hardwicke asked her for an informal screen test. Kristen learned her lines in minutes and totally captivated the director. And from there began the start of Kristen Jaymes Stewart's world domination!

ON JON HEDER, WHO PLAYED NAPOLEON DYNAMITE:
"Oh my God, he's sooo hot. He's a crack up. It would be fun to work with him."

SCHOOL? YOU EITHER LOVE IT OR YOU HATE IT...

Although a lot of child actors find it hard to work while growing up, Kristen loved it. "I didn't have too many problems," she said. "I had to stop going to school because I worked too much ... I got so much out of home schooling. I really loved home school. Independent study is for me." Kristen loves her schooling and is involved in an independent studies correspondence course, where you work at your own speed. "It's actually really easy to get behind!" she says.

But did she miss being at school? Not really. She stopped going to school when she was in seventh grade, and said it was a great reality check. "That whole hierarchy just sort of comes crumbling down and it doesn't mean anything anymore and you find that you don't know a whole lot of people anymore because you really don't care to know them," she says.

She found the popularity aspect of being at school very hard. "If you didn't wear the right pair of jeans – and I was so not that kid – then you were totally scrutinised and persecuted. It would've been so obvious if I tried (to fit in) – my whole family would have looked at me all of a sudden like, 'Why are you a different person?'".

And she's kept some great friends because of leaving school when she did. "In doing that at a really young age, I cemented relationships that really are pretty solid and all

She can sing too! Kristen received praise for her performance of weepie *Into the Wild* (2007), where she also wrote and performed a song on the soundtrack. In fact, she's been playing for years.

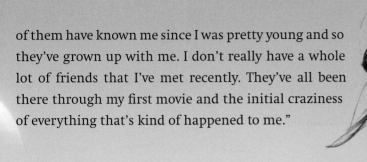

of them have known me since I was pretty young and so they've grown up with me. I don't really have a whole lot of friends that I've met recently. They've all been there through my first movie and the initial craziness of everything that's kind of happened to me."

FAMILY FIRST

Her parents have been a real rock for her too. "They don't sit down and give me pointed advice like 'Kristen, you should do this and this.' They've always been really supportive in that you can drop out of this at any time you want. Basically you just have to make yourself happy and you've got to do what you want to do. And they're just really motivating, sort of a driving force, which is something I really need."

Kristen also feels like she's getting back confidence she had as a child. "When I was little I was so confident and so comfortable in my own skin. I would say anything to anyone. Then you turn 13 and you're really inhibited and insecure. But I think as you get older you get more of that confidence back from when you were younger."

KRISTEN'S HOROSCOPE:

aries

Being Aries, Kristen possesses some typical Aries traits. She is adventurous and energetic, pioneering and courageous, enthusiastic and confident, as well as dynamic and quick-witted. But the ram has a dark side too. Kristen can be selfish, quick-tempered, impulsive, impatient, foolhardy and a bit of a daredevil!

KRISTEN likes

Action
Being first
Challenges
Championing causes
Spontaneity

KRISTEN dislikes

Waiting around
Admitting failure
Authority
Other people's advice

CHAPTER 2

twilight

so what happens?

When Bella Swan's mother remarries, she decides to leave Phoenix, Arizona to live with her father in the rainy little town of Forks in Washington. She meets the mysterious and gorgeous Edward at school, who at first acts like he hates her, but after rescuing her from a late-night encounter with some drunken hooligans, reveals he can't stay away from her any longer and a rather unusual love affair begins. Unusual because Edward has superhuman

Kristen had to wear brown contact lenses for Twilight *(and* New Moon*) because she has naturally green eyes while Bella's eyes are supposed to be brown.*

speed and strength, because his skin glitters like diamonds in the sunlight, because he's been a vampire since 1918, and most importantly because despite being attracted to Bella as his soul mate, he also thirsts for her blood.

Luckily for her, Edward's family have taught themselves to be vegetarian vampires – only feeding on animals, not humans. But he must fight his thirst for her.

Although Bella meets and is for the most part welcomed by Edward's family, when unexpected vampire visitors realise there is a human among the Cullen coven they go out of their way to kill Bella. The film culminates in a fight to save Bella's life. But can the forbidden love between a vampire and a mortal ever succeed?

KRISTEN - BEING BELLA

Kristen was already an experienced actress when she took on the role of Bella, but her starring role in the *Twilight* saga is easily the biggest role of her career to date. And she took it very seriously, determined to represent fully the world that Stephenie Meyer created in her novels.

Kristen felt a total sense of responsibility to the story and to the character of Bella, but this made her task even more difficult. In the books Bella is the person you experience the story of Edward through. "She's not distinct and you don't read her as like, 'Oh, wow. That's a character that I can really sink my teeth into', so you put yourself in that position and so I'm never going to satisfy everyone. I'd be playing the most disjointed character. It's really a self-conscious role. It's entirely Kristen in the situation. I didn't have a really distinct character to play. It's just this girl caught up in an extravagant situation."

As long as she stayed true to the story, Kristen says she didn't mind whether people liked her as the character or not. She says she was attracted to the vampire-romance because it allowed her to embody "this sort of powerful idea of untouchable, superior love." But this meant that Kristen

The worst thing about shooting Twilight*? The unpredictable weather! Some days when the cast and crew were shooting, they would experience rain storms, sunshine, and hail – all within the space of a few hours!*

"Though we were warned, I figured it would be a pretty exclusive fan base. I thought we were making a cult movie; I had no idea it was going to be this, like, phenomenon."

and vampire love interest Robert Pattinson, who played Edward Cullen, felt a lot of pressure to perform. They needn't have worried though. The pair has chemistry that burns hot off the screen – so hot that they have been constantly denying rumours they are an item since *Twilight* was released.

Another challenge that Kristen faced in playing the role of Bella was being clumsy on cue. "I'm far from graceful," she said, "but it's really hard to be clumsy on cue. But I decided that Bella is awkward because she's always so caught up in thinking about other things."

One thing's for sure – Kristen has always been interested in complicated characters and that was what drew her to *Twilight* and the characters of Bella and Edward. "I'm interested in unhealthy, neurotic people," she says. "That's what I found in both of the characters. The power balance is interesting because you have this one really perfect [character] but he's the one who's really afraid and tortured and not confident. He really thinks he should protect this girl and just go away, and she's the sure-footed, strong woman who at the same time is willing to subject herself and give up power which is the most powerful, strong thing you can do ... and I think it's an innately female quality to say 'OK, I don't need this but you can have it, big man.' So I just found it interesting."

ON THE SET AND INTO THE TWILIGHT

Kristen begged for an audition for *Twilight* once she'd read the script, but she also felt uncomfortable with many of the lines she had to say, as she thought they were a little corny. But how much was changed from the original script? "We

changed everything," she says. "There wasn't one scene we didn't touch. There were many occasions, really quiet parts of the movie when it's just Edward and Bella together, where I was like, 'Alright, we're not saying any of the lines. We're just going to do the whole scene with no lines.'"

But Kristen admits that feeling like the lines were corny was just her being self-conscious. "Those wrenching fundamental emotions, I mean how else do you express them? How else do you say, 'I love you'? How else do you say, 'I want to die for you'? I mean, those are really dramatic lines, but when expressed in that context, there really is no other way to say it. Catherine [Hardwicke, director] really helped me with that. She put me in the right position and sort of forced me to go there. You have to be so exposed, so entirely cracked open and vulnerable to be able to give like that. So on the page it was really corny, but we worked it out."

twilight hottie alert:
ROB PATTINSON – EDWARD CULLEN

FULL NAME: Robert Thomas Pattinson

DATE OF BIRTH: 13 May 1986

PLACE OF BIRTH: London, England

CURRENT LOCATION: Rents an apartment in LA, stays at his parents' pad in London and spends time in Vancouver filming

NICKNAMES: Rob, Rpattz, Patty

HEIGHT: 6 feet 1 inch (1.85 m)

RELATIONSHIP STATUS: Single

ROMANTIC RUMOURS: Paris Hilton, Natalie Portman, Rihanna, Miley Cyrus, and any other celebrity who stands within ten feet of him

IDEAL NIGHT: Staying in watching movies, eating fast food and playing his guitar

SPORTS: Rob hates sports and is particularly terrible at baseball

FEAR: Rob is petrified of flying. He says, "I don't deal with it I just spend the whole flight freaking out."

BEST QUALITIES: According to best friend Sam Bradley, he's a great cook, and is just so tidy, he's a neat freak!

FAVOURITE FOOD: If you wanted to take Rob on a date you should go for an In-N-Out Burger. He loves them! He's also addicted to Diet Coke and Cinnamon Toast Crunch

MEET ROB!

Best known for playing Cedric Diggory in *Harry Potter and the Goblet of Fire*, many *Twilight* fans were shocked at the fact that he was chosen to play Edward Cullen. There was rebellion on the *Twilight* message boards, with many Twi-hards saying the movie had already been ruined because of Rob. But needless to say, after the movie came out, they soon changed their minds!

Like Kristen, Rob has spent some time on the internet looking for things people say about him since he started filming *Twilight*. "I admit I do look for myself sometimes. I used to do it a lot more before. Now I only look at the negative stuff. I just want to know whoever's saying negative stuff, I want to remember their names. I write it all down in my black book." He says the internet feeds the worst part of your soul, when you have nothing to do and you're too tired to read a book. "I'll read the news, you go on to the New York Times, you get bored and go on IMDb. Then you realise how pathetic you are. I have to delete my history. It is kind of addictive, but at the same time pathetic."

Although Rob found it difficult to find a focus at school, he's changed his attitude since winning the role of Edward. He spent months alone preparing for the role, isolating himself from friends and family and writing journal entries in character as Edward, as he really didn't want to let fans down. To help him, Stephenie Meyer gave Rob the draft of a manuscript of *Twilight* which she had written not from Bella's point of view, but from Edward's.

So does Rob see any similarities between him and Edward? "I think I'm quite similar in his bad points," he

says, "I mean I'm quite possessive, and a bit of a loner. But his good points, I'm not that polite. I'm kind of polite, sort of, but I'm not that similar I don't think."

ROB, DATING AND ROMANCE

Although he's become a globally renowned heart-throb almost overnight, Rob wasn't always such a hit with the ladies. "I had really bad luck with girls in high school," he says. "The ones I liked hated me and the ones that liked me were not my type. But that's something that I still go through. I like girls that I shouldn't like. But I'm learning and now I take my time before I let the girl know."

Although he might be single, meeting girls was the reason that Rob got into acting in the first place! His dad got him psyched about the movie industry by first joining amateur productions at Barnes Theatre Company. "He saw a bunch of pretty girls who were going to it," Rob confesses. "[He] said: 'Hey Rob, you've got to go to that.' That's the reason I still do it!"

He might claim he's not romantic, but Rob once took a girl to Cornwall for the weekend. He admits that they stayed in a 'dump' and that he forgot to mention that he'd been given the train tickets for free. Given the company, we're sure we wouldn't mind!

Rob's other notable date stories run along the same line: "I had a date with a girl at the zoo. But, we didn't have enough money to pay the entrance. So, we ran along the fence of the zoo on the outside. It was raining and we didn't have an umbrella with us. I think that was romantic."

"The best thing he knows how to do is opening a bottle of beer!" **KRISTEN JOKES ABOUT ROB'S KITCHEN ABILITIES**

"When I met Kristen, there was instant chemistry. She brought something out of me that I can't even explain."
ROB PATTINSON, ON HIS BOND WITH KRISTEN STEWART

He's been romantically linked with almost every eligible female in Hollywood, as well as some not eligible ones – like Kristen Stewart! In fact, rumours about the two being an item have persisted ever since *Twilight* came out, despite the fact that Kristen has a boyfriend. But Rob doesn't care about the rumours. "I don't really care about it. I have the same little set of friends and I don't have anyone who would really get affected adversely [by false rumours]. Every single person who they sort of romantically link me to … I just don't even really know anyone. So it doesn't really affect me that much."

One thing he's not used to is being surrounded by so many fans. "It's a weird experience! You do tend to start getting a little bit paranoid about stuff. Looking around when you're walking down the street, in case you get mobbed by teenage girls!"

A DATE WITH DESTINY

As soon as she read the lines with him, Kristen knew Rob was perfect for the role of Edward Cullen. "I got hardcore pain from Rob. Not that he's in pain now, but he definitely had that going on and that's what Edward needs. It was purely just connection."

Director Catherine Hardwicke had a couple of other Edwards in mind, but Kristen was adamant that Rob had to get the part. "I was like, 'Are you joking? I can't do the movie unless Rob does it.'"

Nobody can fail to have realised the chemistry the pair have onscreen. There was a lot of pressure on the pair to make sure the kissing scenes really delivered, as

these scenes have to communicate a sense of the couple developing an entire relationship. "They can't just make out. They can't just kiss each other like normal people," says Kristen. Looks like the pair worked super-hard to get it right – apparently in the main kissing scene in Bella's bedroom, Rob got so carried away he fell off the bed!

They might not be an item, but Kristen has nothing but praise for her *Twilight* co-star. "He's so good and he's so soulful and he's just not a liar — you can feel pain from him," Stewart says. "The cool thing about the story is that it's a seemingly wonderful fantasy — let's fall in love with vampires and live forever — but it's so much harder than that. Imagine living forever. Living one life is hard enough."

Acting the part

The movie *Twilight* required most of the actors to transform themselves physically in some way. Kristen wore hairpieces and Taylor Lautner wore a wig. Nikki Reed (Rosalie) was supposed to wear a wig as her character is blonde but she decided at the last minute to dye her hair instead. But it took 36 hours for the hair stylists to turn Nikki's hair blonde! Nikki had been living in Hawaii for three months prior to shooting *Twilight*, so she started a rigorous regime of exfoliating, trying to get rid of her tan, as vampires aren't supposed to be tanned!

Originally Rob was supposed to wear a wig too as the director wanted Edward to have long hair but Rob protested so much she changed her mind. Thank goodness he complained – his natural hair totally makes his look!

CHAPTER 3

new moon

"The term 'new moon' refers to the phase of the moon opposite a full moon. It is when the sun is on the opposite side of the moon from us and thus the bright side of the moon is not visible from earth. This is the darkest kind of night. New Moon is the darkest period of Bella's life."
Author, Stephenie Meyer

so what happens?

After Bella recovers from the vampire attack that almost killed her in *Twilight*, she celebrates her birthday with Edward and his family. When a paper cut results in Bella's blood being shed, she is nearly attacked by Edward's brother, Jasper, the newest member of the family who is still adapting to the 'vegetarian' vampire lifestyle.

To protect Bella, Edward ends the relationship and his family leave Forks. Broken-hearted, Bella resorts to reckless pursuits like motorbiking, (finding that adrenaline makes her hallucinate about Edward), and she also grows closer to childhood friend Jacob Black, who has transformed into quite a hottie. She is also having constant nightmares, eerie dream sequences in which Edward keeps appearing.

Bella is being hunted by evil vampire Victoria, and it is up to Jacob – a werewolf – and the rest of the Quileute Indian werewolves to protect Bella. In the meantime, Edward is distraught at the prospect of eternity without Bella and leaves for Italy, hoping to persuade the Volturi – a powerful vampire coven that impose the laws of the vampire world – to kill him. Edward's sister Alice rushes with Bella to Italy to try to change Edward's mind, but will they make it in time – and can Bella choose between vampire and werewolf, now her loyalties have been tested to the limit?

BEHIND THE SCENES

The second film in the Twilight series, *New Moon* was directed by Chris Weitz, who directed *About a Boy* and *The Golden Compass*. Weitz replaced Catherine Hardwicke, who directed *Twilight* but pulled out of *New Moon* due to scheduling conflicts. *New Moon* was shot in Vancouver and Montepulciano in Italy, and filming for the movie began in early 2009.

Bringing in a whole new set of hunks for *New Moon* – the wolf pack – was no easy task. Director Chris Weitz was so determined to be authentic to the novel that each member

WOLFPACK FACT:
Members of the wolf pack went through "wolf camp" together, to get buff and bond with each other. Now there's a camp we'd like a place on …

You might have seen the cast hanging out in the Glowbal Grill and Satay Bar in Yaletown. They went there to eat a few times a week while they were filming.

of the wolf pack had to have papers proving their Native American Indian descent. The wolf pack also had to film almost entirely in the nude for nearly all their scenes!

But Chris Weitz did permit one significant change between the novel and the film, something that everyone was pleased about: the presence of Edward. While in the book Bella just hears his voice in her head, in the movie, flittering images of Edward appear throughout, much to the relief of Rob Pattinson fans the world over. And isn't that everybody?

Filming for *New Moon* required a lot of early mornings and late nights. Sometimes filming didn't finish until 6am. But whatever the time and whatever the weather, the cast was always met by armies of fans who had been patiently waiting in the rain to catch a glimpse of their heroes!

The cast had an awesome time hanging out together on set. Ashley Greene who plays Alice Cullen said the second movie was a much more fun and less stressful experience for all the actors, as they had their bearings and knew what was expected of them.

Perhaps that's why they were always out for coffee or meeting in bars or for dinner! Cast members even found time to listen to some live music, as Kristen and Rob went to support Rob's friend Sam Bradley who was performing at a charity gig. Rumour had it that afterwards, they went out partying with Sam Bradley into the early hours of the morning. The cast also hung out at Jackson Rathbone's 100 Monkeys (the band he plays in) show.

The set was rife with supposed script leaks that appeared on Twitter, and love and romance rumours that persisted about Kristen and Rob, despite the fact that Kristen was pictured around the set with long-term boyfriend Michael Angarano. Taylor Lautner was seen spending an awful lot of time with Selena Gomez – they saw each other almost every day, going bowling and staying in watching DVDs, just hanging out. Aw. Although fear not ladies, he still claims to be single...

VAMPIRE FACT:

There was one cast member who seemed to be more suited to the vampire life than the others – Peter Facinelli, who plays bloodsucking father figure Dr. Carlisle Cullen, and who loved the night shoots. "Everybody else is [tired] by like two, three in the morning, which is weird because I'm the old guy! They should be the ones that should be like party hardy all night long," jokes the 35-year-old of his young co-stars who range from 17-23. "At five in the morning I was like, 'I could go another 10 hours!' And they were like, 'Crash!' "

new moon playlist

Is your iPod totally *Twilight*? When Stephenie Meyer was writing *New Moon*, she was listening to these songs as representing part of the story from a particular character's point of view. Can you work out which of these songs could belong to Bella, Jacob or Edward?

1. "Do You Realize?" The Flaming Lips
2. "Paper Cut" Linkin Park
3. "Hyper Music" Muse
4. "Apocalypse Please" Muse
5. "Time Stands Still" The All-American Rejects
6. "Empty Room" Marjorie Fair
7. "Unwell" Matchbox Twenty
8. "Pain" Jimmy Eat World
9. "Ride" The Vines
10. "Fix You" Coldplay
11. "Blueside" Rooney
12. "Over My Head (Cable Car)" The Fray
13. "Going Under" Evanescence
14. "Tautou" Brand New
15. "Be My Escape" Relient K
16. "Never Let You Down" Verve Pipe
17. "Sing For Absolution" Muse
18. "Ya Mamma" Fatboy Slim
19. "D.O.A." Foo Fighters
20. "Stare" Marjorie Fair
21. "Memory" Sugarcult
22. "The Truth About Heaven" Armor For Sleep
23. "The Scientist" Coldplay
24. "Sound of Pulling Heaven Down" Blue October

ANOTHER FILM, ANOTHER YEAR, ANOTHER BIRTHDAY

Celebrating her birthday onset has become something of a tradition for Kristen. She celebrated her 18th birthday last year while filming *Twilight* (she had a cake and everything!), and this year, while filming *New Moon*, she celebrated her 19th birthday.

This time she and some pals hit up a private room in a restaurant for a late night celebration, including Nikki Reed and a friend, Taylor Lautner, Robert Pattinson, his friend Sam, and Jackson Rathbone. Rumour has it that Taylor left first, but then at the end of the night, Kristen and Jackson took off together while the others got into a cab separately, and didn't meet up with the birthday girl again. Wonder what all these midnight party-goers were up to?!

MOBBED BY FANS

While leaving a book signing in spring 2009, Kristen Stewart had to be rescued from a huge crowd of *Twilight* fans. Kristen was dragged out of the crowd by security and thrown in a van for her own safety. While Kristen only says it was "a really surreal experience", it sounds pretty scary! Thankfully that bad experience hasn't put her off meeting her fans. Phew!

LIVING UP TO THE HYPE

No stranger to controversy over the films, Kristen shocked fans by saying she wouldn't have signed up to play Bella if she'd known how popular *Twilight* was going to be. But as she explained later, she said it during a moment of insecurity.

"Having people expecting so much about you is not nice. But I believe I would've done it anyway. A phenomenon like this can be overwhelming, but at the same time it doesn't affect me at all. It doesn't change my real life," she later said.

She added modestly: "They scream for Bella, the character, who could've been anybody. People are really obsessed with Rob. However, I'm used to being in movies that nobody watches."

Despite all the hype, Kristen is determined to keep her feet on the ground: "Fame doesn't affect my life. Fame is not real."

new moon hot property:
TAYLOR LAUTNER

FULL NAME: Taylor Daniel Lautner

DATE OF BIRTH: 11 February 1992

PLACE OF BIRTH: Grand Rapids, Michigan, USA

HEIGHT: 5 feet 10 inches (1.79 m)

SPORT: loves playing football and baseball, enjoys watching college football and supports the Michigan Wolverines

PETS: A Maltese named Roxy

DANCING: he performs with a hip-hop dance group and a jazz dance group

DON'T MESS WITH TAYLOR: he's a world champion in martial arts!

TRANSFORMING TAYLOR

Taylor Lautner almost didn't make it into *New Moon*. At first, the movie's makers thought they might have to recast the role, as there is such a physical transformation in Jacob between the first and second novels, they didn't think Taylor would be able to take it on. But he was determined to make the role his own, working out everyday and putting on 30 pounds of muscle!

So after months of speculation, the novel's author Stephenie Meyer confirmed that Taylor Lautner would be reprising his role as Jacob Black, and thousands of girls around the world cheered for the good news.

On set Taylor was super busy, shooting scenes almost everyday and continuing his gruelling workout routine. Given his young age, Taylor has been lucky enough to have his dad around the entire time (it's law to have a guardian on the job when you're Taylor's age). So perhaps that's why he was so well behaved - everyone who worked with him said he was sweet, polite, grateful, and worked hard. Actually, perhaps it's just because he's such a great, grounded guy.

Taylor was really popular with his co-stars in a little brother way - Kristen and Nikki Reed were super protective of him, and also both intent on helping him, whenever possible, to gain more of the spotlight. Making Taylor famous is almost like a project for them - but with those smouldering looks and super-nice personality - it doesn't look like he needs much help at all.

42

CHAPTER 4

style & fashion

You can't have failed to notice the change in Kristen Stewart's style over the course of her acting career. From one pair of pyjamas for a whole movie in *Panic Room* to hippy threads in *Into the Wild* to her low-key prep-indie look in *Twilight*, one thing's for certain – her characters' wardrobes are definitely varied.

"Beauty is subjective. If you go online and google "the ugliest girl in the world" you'll get my picture. Believe me, it's everywhere. A lot of people think I'm hideous"

KRISTEN ON THE HATERS

KRISTEN LOVES THESE LOOKS:

🍎 Plain black t shirt

🍎 Skinny jeans

🍎 Tank top

🍎 Converse

Kristen herself has taken on the role of fashion icon after being more of a tomboy and not that into clothes when she was younger. "It's such a bizarre thing, to me, to consider that what I wear, what I do with my hair, affects my career. I'm not the type of person who has a million things in my closet," she says. Instead of shopping for quantity, she works with a stylist to find classy pieces that work for different occasions.

kristen's style

Kristen's quirky tomboy style often gives way to classy night-time looks.

One of her most lauded outfits was the asymmetrical dress she wore for the LA *Twilight* premiere.

Recently she's taken to wearing short mini-dresses showing off her great pins. She likes wearing dresses with pockets, bold animal prints, and wearing unusual combinations of text, like leather with lace.

For a girl who seems most comfortable in Converse she's not afraid of sky high heels either!

FAVOURITE DESIGNER:
Chanel

"I've always had an aversion to looking sexy but I've grown out of it"
KRISTEN ON HER
NEW MATURE LOOK

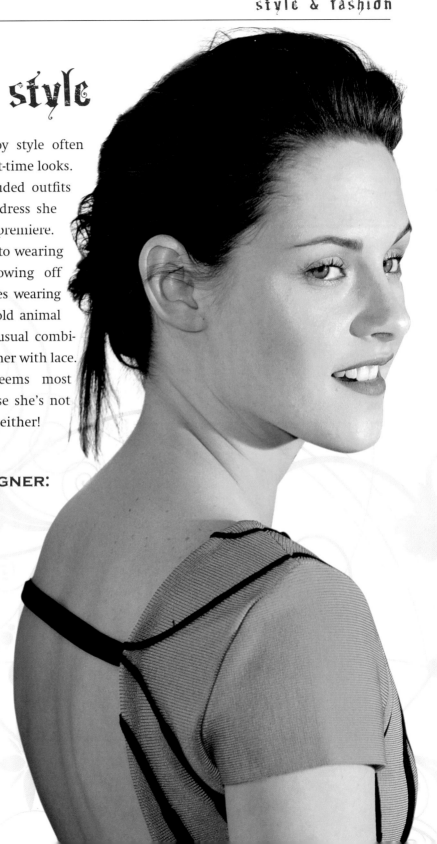

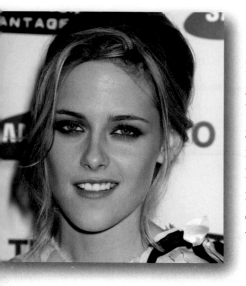

NATURAL IS BEST

Kristen likes to keep it simple. When you've got skin that good, well-tamed brows and eyes so beautiful, minimal is best. She likes a smudge of black kohl around her eyes to give her that smoking-hot look, a slick of mascara and a raspberry stain for those lovely lips. To attain the make-up-less look, use blot powder to even out any patches on the face. Kristen doesn't maintain any kind of excessive skin care routine, just washing and moisturising every night before bed. Lucky girl!

ALTERNATIVE CHIC

Lucky enough to be blessed with long thick brown curls, Kristen likes experimenting with her hair up in loose twists, or flowing freely about her face. Her must-have hair items are straighteners and curling tongs, for those days when her tresses just won't do what they're told. She also likes keeping her hair colour fresh by dying it every year: from blonde, to mousy, to dark brown, to red, to vampish black! And she's not one for overdoing it. Kristen is regularly seen on the red carpet with hair that looks like she's just rolled out of bed – a bit grungy, a bit bed-head, but 100% alternative chic.

VINTAGE CLOTHES: *"Anything that's beat up. I kind of like to look like a hobo."*

To get the Kristen look, try twisting your just-washed hair into loose plaits before bedtime, then shaking the plaits loose in the morning and using just a little wax to twist the ends.

bella's style

Since *Twilight* Bella became such a fashion icon that we were rushing to the stores to find ourselves jeans and jacket combos and Jansport rucksacks just like hers.

The gutsy heroine rocks one look, but boy, does she do it well: classic tomboy chic. She favours dark blue jeans

that are pencil leg shaped, a style that is both timeless and on-trend. Of course, because it's always raining in Forks, Bella needs to cover up with a casual jacket. While she was wearing BB Dakota, surfwear label Billabong is also high on her fashion list. The jacket needs to be charcoal grey and have pockets for our heroine to store her pepper spray.

Bella's look is finished with a horizontally striped woolly jumper or green button shirt. And voila! Your transformation is complete!

COMPLETING THE LOOK

Achieving Bella's look required more than just some new threads. Stephenie Meyer's description of Bella in the books was with large, chocolate-brown eyes, meaning Kristen had to wear brown contact lenses every day.

The biggest challenge on the set was the rain. The cast were outside all the time, and it rained the entire time they were there. Most of the shots were exterior, and trying to fix make-up in the rain with wet faces and wet brushes was difficult. The experience made Jeanne Van Phue, the film's make-up artist, convert to SK-II AirTouch make-up, which goes on flawlessly and – as she discovered on set – is water resistant!

It wasn't just eyes and make-up. Like co-star Taylor Lautner, Kristen also wore hairpieces in the film, to save valuable time each day because she didn't have to keep doing her hair.

CHAPTER 5
love & romance

rumours!

Since shooting began for Twilight, rumours have abounded about Kristen Stewart and her hot-to-trot onscreen vampire love interest, Rob Pattinson. Although the pair denied this from the start, the rumours continue – with many Twi-hards hoping that their real life Bella and Edward really will end up together.

In real life, Kristen has a boyfriend that isn't Rob! She met long-term squeeze Michael Angarano in 2004 when they appeared in the movie *Speak*, but they only began

dating two years ago. "He's older than me – he's 20 now – but when you're 13 and he's turning 16, it was always sort of an out-of-reach thing. Then you get a little older and realise, what am I thinking? I can have you like that!" She laughs, snapping her fingers.

And Kristen is very happy with Michael, who has come to visit her on-set numerous times. "He's awesome." When he comes to visit, they like to go for sushi together and just hang out. For one of his trips to see her while she was filming *New Moon*, he arranged a romantic weekend together at a different hotel with an ocean view, so they could escape from the crowds. What a sweetie!

tensions

But while things between her and Michael continue to be fine, the rumour mill continues to grind. Allegedly, Kristen was reprimanded by the studio for photos of her with boyfriend Michael Angarano in Vancouver on the set of *New Moon*. Rumour has it that the fact that Kristen loves someone other than "Edward Cullen" is hard for many Twi-hard fans to accept, so many think the studio have decided it is in their best interest to keep up this illusion.

DOES KRISTEN BELIEVE IN LOVE AT FIRST SIGHT?

"I've never been interested in anybody I ever thought was attractive when I first looked at them. It happens like a second later. If they're not looking at me, I'm like pshh. When somebody looks at you a certain way, it's like it's indescribable. I've never been the type of girl who has looked for this unattainable thing that isn't aware of you. I've never been fixated on anything that wasn't like fixated on me" [laughs]

WHY DOES SHE THINK VAMPIRES ARE SO SEXY?

"I think they're classic. They're made to draw you in so you'll fall on their claws, and when they get you, they'll bite you. You let yourself be wrapped by their charms, they're like the forbidden fruit."

So Summit has supposedly told Kristen to be more careful when she's in public with Michael (particularly around the paparazzi, as several teams of photographers from different agencies camped outside her hotel every day), stressing that, at least during filming, they'd actually prefer that he not come around at all. It's also been suggested that Summit isn't pleased with the closeness between Robert Pattinson and Nikki Reed. Eek!

the future

Kristen admits she's always thought of herself as awkward when it comes to love, much like Bella. "I don't think I'm ever going to not fumble around. I think that's just life. That's how you live life is you fumble around."

Now she's hit superstardom, Kristen maintains it is super important to her to maintain her relationships. "The hardest thing in life is to maintain personal relationships and to feel like they're real and genuine. You're always going to have expectations that you're trying to meet and you just have to roll with it." Good job Kristen's boyfriend Michael is an actor too, and understands the pressure the *Twilight* star is under.

ON HER RELATIONSHIP WITH ROB PATTINSON

"Rob and I are good friends. We went through a lot together, so we feel very close. But if we go out in public, every little detail is scrutinised, like the way I stand next to him. And it's like, I know this guy really well [laughs]. It's only natural that we're sort of leaning on each other, because we're put in the most psychotic situations."

CHAPTER 6
looking ahead

With so many talents – acting, singing, playing guitar – and so much ambition, it's a dead cert that Kristen Stewart is one feisty, independent starlet who's going to be around for a long time to come.

Kristen is cracking on with production of *Eclipse*, the third instalment of the *Twilight* saga, which is being directed by David Slade but retains the same screenwriter, Melissa Rosenberg. The story picks up in Seattle, where Bella is torn between her love for Edward and her friendship with Jacob, as well as trying not to end up as dinner for vengeful Victoria. Twi-hards are also excited about rumours that there may be a big screen adaption of *Breaking Dawn* too, the fourth and final book in the *Twilight* series, although how they will create Bella's child – a baby with a full set of teeth and the mind of a 22 year old – will be a challenge for them, for sure!

THE RUNAWAYS

Other new projects for Kristen include taking on the role of original female rocker Joan Jett in a movie of *The Runaways*. In preparation for the role, Kristen hung out a lot with Joan Jett, who produced the movie. Kristen was in awe of Joan, saying: "She's a badass. She's like the ultimate cool and like really deep too. She's very thoughtful ... She's very thoughtful and she loves what she does. She cares about so many people. She's an activist. She's really amazing." It's a good job Kristen likes to keep busy. With only eight weeks break between shooting *New Moon* and *Eclipse* to squeeze *The Runaways* into, they'll be plenty for her to sink her teeth into!

Although she always wanted to go to college – namely Sydney University in Australia, where her mum is from – recently, Kristen has changed her mind. "I thought about it for a while, but I have a problem with authority," the feisty chick says. "I don't like people telling me what to read. I'll have an education independently."

While the media might have twisted her words to make it seem like she hates *Twilight*, actually, that's not the case at all. She's glad she got the part of Bella Swan, as it means she won't have to fight for parts anymore. "It makes it so much easier, I don't have to fight to get into a movie that I really want to do. It's not a fight anymore, and it was. It's been really good for me, only good."

K-11

Coming from a showbiz family like she does, perhaps it was only a matter of time before Kristen took on a job with a family member. Kristen and Nikki Reed have parts in a movie that Kristen's mum, Jules, wrote and is directing, called *K-11*. "It takes place in a dorm of the LA County Jail. It's like where you go if you can't be put into general population. So it's full of eccentric, crazy, off-the-wall characters, and me and Nikki play two of them," says Kristen. "Jason Mewes wakes up in this place and doesn't know where he is and tries to break out for two weeks. He tries to integrate himself into the community. It's a really sweet but really screwed up little family in there."

shining star

But Kristen is adamant about one thing: while she loves acting, she doesn't want to act forever. "My family has always been involved in films so I really feel like making movies. I want to make movies ... I'm not as much of a story-teller as I am just a lover of words, putting them together, so I think I'd rather write short stories and maybe, who knows, I would love to write a novel."

With so much planned in her immediate future, it's a wonder she'll have time to sleep! Perhaps there are benefits to being a vampire, after all ...

IF SHE HAD TO CHOOSE A VAMPIRE, WHICH ONE WOULD IT BE?

"Well, if I had to choose between the characters of the movie, I would choose Edward because I know he wouldn't hurt me."

PICTURE CREDITS

Getty: 4, 6, 8, 12 (background), 16, 18 (background), 21 (background),
26, 30, 34 (background), 36, 38, 42, 45, 47, 48 (background), 50, 52
(background), 58 (background), 63
Rex: 2, 10, 23, 24, 28, 31, 32, 34, 35, 40, 44, 48, 52, 53, 55, 60
PA Photos: 7, 12, 13, 14, 18, 21, 25, 37, 39, 46, 56, 58, 59

ACKNOWLEDGEMENTS

Josie Rusher would like to thank Helia Phoenix, Amanda Harris,
Helen Ewing, James Martindale, Jane Sturrock, Frank Brinkley,
Briony Hartley and Rich Carr.

First published in hardback in
Great Britain in 2009 by
Orion Books an imprint of the
Orion Publishing Group Ltd
Orion House, 5 Upper St Martin's Lane
London WC2H 9EA
An Hachette UK Company

10 9 8 7 6 5 4 3 2 1

A CIP catalogue record for this book is available
from the British Library.

ISBN: 978 1 4091 1381 2

Designed by Goldust Design
Printed in Spain by Cayfosa

The Orion Publishing Group's policy is to use
papers that are natural, renewable and recyclable
and made from wood grown in sustainable forests.
The logging and manufacturing processes are
expected to conform to the environmental
regulations of the country of origin.

Every effort has been made to fulfil requirements
with regard to reproducing copyright material.
The author and publisher will be glad to rectify
any omissions at the earliest opportunity.

www.orionbooks.co.uk